W9-DFR-064

NEW VANGUARD 215

PANZER 38(t)

STEVEN J. ZALOGA   ILLUSTRATED BY RICHARD CHASEMORE

First published in Great Britain in 2014 by Osprey Publishing,

PO Box 883, Oxford, OX1 9PL, UK

PO Box 3985, New York, NY 10185-3985, USA

E-mail: info@ospreypublishing.com

Osprey Publishing is part of the Osprey Group

A CIP catalog record for this book is available from the British Library

Print ISBN: 978 1 78200 395 3

PDF ebook ISBN: 978 1 78200 396 0

ePub ebook ISBN: 978 1 78200 397 7

Index by Angela Hall

Typeset in Sabon and Myriad Pro

Originated by PDQ Media, Bungay, UK

Printed in China through Worldprint Ltd

14 15 16 17 18   10 9 8 7 6 5 4 3 2 1

Osprey Publishing is supporting the Woodland Trust, the UK's leading woodland conservation charity, by funding the dedication of trees.

www.ospreypublishing.com

AUTHOR'S NOTE

The author would like to acknowledge the help of the late Ivan Bajtos and Janusz Magnuski in providing him with photos and references that were used in this book. Thanks also go to Just Probst and Lee Ness for reference help on this project.

Glossary

Abt.	Abteilung: German army unit between regiment and battalion
Ausf.	Ausführung: version (German)
Bef.Wg.	Befelswagen: command vehicle (German)
BMM	Böhmisch-Mährische Maschinenfabrik AG: Bohemia-Moravia Industrial Plant, German name for ČKD after 1939 occupation
BP	Behelfsmäßiger Panzerzug: armored train (German)
ČKD	Českomoravská-Kolben-Daněk
Heeresgruppe	Army Group: a formation with several field armies (German)
LT	Lekhý Tank: Light Tank (Czech)
PzBef	Panzer Befelswagen: command tank (German)
PzKpfw	Panzerkampfwagen: armored combat vehicle; tank (German)
Pzgr.Ptr.	Panzergranate Patronen: antitank round (German)
Pzw	Panzerwagen: tank (Swiss German)
(t)	tschechoslowakischen: Czechoslovak (German)
vz.	Vzor: model (Czech)
Waffenamt	Wehrmacht Weapons Department
Zug	Platoon (German)

Title page image: A PzKpfw 38(t) Ausf. B during training exercises at Truppenübungsplatz Baumholder on April 2, 1940. This is a Zugführer tank, evident from the armored plate covering the hull machine-gun opening. This was necessary to provide enough space in the hull for the Fu 2 and Fu 5 radio transceiver.

CONTENTS

INTRODUCTION   **4**
- Export Tank Origins
- Czechoslovak Army Requirement

INTO GERMAN SERVICE   **10**
- Combat debut
- Early Revisions

TECHNICAL DESCRIPTION   **13**
- 37mm KwK 38(t) gun antitank performance
- PzKpfw 38(t) Variants

GLORY DAYS IN FRANCE   **16**

LATE-PRODUCTION VERSIONS   **20**

THE SWEDISH DIVERSION   **24**

BATTLES ON THE RUSSIAN FRONT   **24**
- Durability and losses of German tank types, Aug–Sep 1941

FINAL PzKpfw 38(t) PRODUCTION TYPES   **28**
- German PzKpfw 38(t) deployment and losses

THE DECLINE OF THE PzKpfw 38(t)   **30**
- Swansong of the PzKpfw 38(t): *Fall Blau*
- Anti-Partisan Tanks
- *Festung Drehtürm*
- Panzer 38 (t) *Drehtürm* deployment
- Next Generation: PzKfw 38(t) n.A.

EXPORT PzKpfw 38(t)   **41**
- Sweden
- Slovakia
- Hungary
- Romania
- Bulgaria

POSTWAR CZECHOSLOVAK SERVICE   **46**

FURTHER READING   **47**

INDEX   **48**

PANZER 38(t)

INTRODUCTION

Originally designed for the army of the Shah of Persia by an émigré Russian engineer, the PzKpfw 38(t) was the only tank of foreign origin to remain in production for the Wehrmacht throughout World War II. When Germany occupied the Czech provinces in 1939, it inherited the small but sophisticated Czech tank industry. The best of the new Czech tanks, the LT 38, was an essential ingredient in enlarging the panzer force in 1939–41. The majority of German tanks were armed with inadequate machine guns and 20mm cannon, but the Czech tanks offered an excellent 37mm gun. The PzKpfw 38(t) proved to be a reliable and effective tank during the Blitzkrieg campaigns of 1939–41, making up nearly a fifth of the panzer force. Its combat effectiveness diminished rapidly after 1941 when confronted with the new generation of Soviet tanks such as the T-34 and KV. Besides its use by German tank units, the PzKpfw 38(t) and its relatives were widely exported and served in a diverse selection of armies including neutrals such as Sweden and Switzerland, as well as with Germany's allies such as Hungary and Romania. It was

This PzKpfw 38(t) Ausf. E is preserved at the Memorial Museum at Poklonna Gora outside Moscow.

withdrawn from front-line German service by 1943, but it remained in use in secondary roles such as anti-partisan units. Manufacture of the tank version of the PzKpfw 38(t) ended in the summer of 1942, but the chassis remained in production throughout the war for a variety of self-propelled guns and tank destroyers. This book deals with the tank variants of this prolific model.

Export Tank Origins

When the Austro-Hungarian Empire collapsed in 1918, the newly independent Czechoslovakia inherited a substantial arms industry. Since the domestic market for armaments was so limited, Czechoslovak firms pursued the international armament business. In the 1930s, Czechoslovakia often ranked third in the world after Britain and France. By this time there were two firms involved in the tank business, the well-known armament firm Škoda in Plzen (Pilsen) and the newcomer, ČKD (Českomoravská-Kolben-Daněk) formed in Praga (Prague) in 1927. ČKD's first big program was the licensed manufacture of the British Carden-Loyd Mk. VI tankette in modified form for the Czechoslovak Army as the Tančik vz. 30. It was followed by the LT vz. 34 light tank, roughly in the category of the Vickers 6-ton tank, with 44 purchased by the Czechoslovak Army. The LT abbreviation means "Lekhý Tank" (Light Tank). Although offered for export, no foreign sales were made.

The principal design engineer at ČKD was an émigré Russian, Alexej Surin, who had migrated to Czechoslovakia in the wake of the Russian Civil War. His first successful export design was the Praga AH-IV tankette. Although called a tankette, it was significantly larger than Carden-Loyd types, and was fitted with a small turret. This new type also pioneered the large road-wheel design that would become a hallmark of Surin's later light tanks. Although the large road wheels might be mistaken for a Christie-type suspension, in fact the Surin design used a bogie consisting of twin road wheels pivoting on a single horizontal spring rather than the individual vertical springs of the famous Christie tanks. ČKD enjoyed its first export success with this tankette, agreeing to sell 30 AH-IVs to the Persian Army (Iranian after 1935). This sale proved vital to the future of the company, as it led to a succession of export orders including those from Romania and Sweden.

With the AH-IV program underway, ČKD also began work on a modernized light tank incorporating the new suspension design. The TNH light tank was intended to compete against the Vickers 6-ton tank in the export market. It won its first export success at the same time as the AH-IV, with an Iranian order in May 1935. The TNH light tank was armed with a Škoda 37mm A4 Beta gun as well as two machine guns, and had a 15mm armor basis. In total, 50 TNH tanks were built for Iran at ČKD's Slaný plant, with delivery completed in May 1937.

The ancestor of the PzKpfw 38(t) was the TNH light tank, with 50 manufactured for the Iranian Army in 1937. There are few details on whether they took part in the fighting with the British and Soviet armies following the August 25, 1941 invasion of Iran.

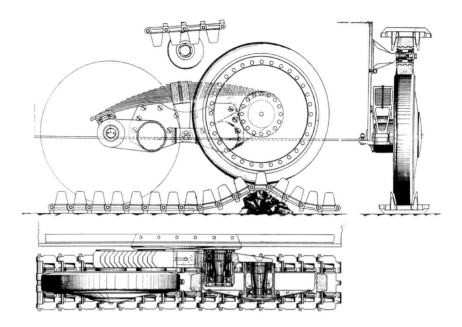

The LT vz. 38 family used an advanced suspension bogie based on two large road wheels mated to a central spring and arm.

The Iranian tanks were deployed in the new Imperial Mechanized Brigade formed in Tehran. It consisted of three regiments: the 1st Antiaircraft Regiment equipped with 75mm Bofors guns towed by Marmon-Herrington trucks, the 2nd AFV Regiment, and the 3rd Mechanized Infantry Regiment. The 2nd Regiment was based on three battalions: a light-tank battalion with the AH-IV tankettes, a medium-tank battalion with the LTH light tanks, and an armored-car squadron with a dozen Marmon-Herrington armored cars. The history of the Mechanized Brigade is obscure. A 1940 Indian Army intelligence report offered a disparaging view of its military effectiveness: "The tanks are seldom seen except on the day of the Annual Review when the Brigade is smartly turned out. The personnel are indifferently trained and the tanks are badly driven across country, being frequently stalled at obstacles." The Brigade would appear to have been intended to serve as a palace guard for the Pahlavi dynasty in Tehran. It is not known if it was involved in any of the fighting following the British–Soviet invasion of August 25, 1941. Nor is it clear whether the tanks took part in the separatist civil war in 1946. The LTH remained in service well into the 1950s.

The new LTH design proved to be a success in the export market, attracting attention from several armies. The Spanish Civil War demonstrated the vital role of tanks on the modern battlefield, and there was a binge of re-armament in Europe. Since several of the potential clients expressed interest in a somewhat lighter and less expensive tank, ČKD developed a derivative with lighter armor.

The firm signed several export orders in quick succession in 1937. On May 27, 1937, the Latvian Army ordered 21 LTL tanks in the lighter configuration and armed with 20mm Oerlikon cannon. In the event, Latvia later switched its order to the heavier LTH configuration, but the Soviet occupation in March 1940 put an end to the program before the tanks could be delivered. As will be detailed later, these ended up in the Slovak Army.

The prewar designs gradually evolved closer and closer to the eventual LT-38 design. This is one of the prototypes of the Peruvian LTP undergoing trials in Czechoslovakia, showing the elongated turret bustle adopted in this version. It was armed with the A3 37mm gun as on the earlier LT-35.

The next order came from South America. In 1933, tanks were used for the first time in South America during the Gran Chaco War between Bolivia and Paraguay. This prompted the Peruvian Army to establish a tank force. After studying several designs, in 1937 Peru selected a version of the initial Latvian LTL design. Called the LTP (P = Peru) by ČKD and the Tanque 39 by Peru, a prototype was delivered to Peru in the autumn of 1938. Peru eventually received 24 LTP tanks through March 1939. A few were used in July 1938, suppressing a military coup d'état in Lima. A company of these tanks was used in combat during the July 1941 border dispute with Ecuador. Curiously

Switzerland obtained 12 LTL-H tanks from Czechoslovakia in May 1939 in the midst of the German occupation, and locally manufactured a further 12. This is tank number 18 that is preserved in Thun at the Swiss Army tank school.

After the war, one of the Swiss Panzerwagen 39 was re-armed with the 47mm Pak 41 gun in a modified turret as a way to extend the useful service life of the tank. However, the program was eventually rejected and the tanks retired.

enough, two of the tank commanders were Czechs who had arrived in Peru to serve as trainers and advisers. The LTP tanks proved very popular in Peruvian service. During World War II, the United States provided 30 M3 Stuart light tanks, but the Peruvian Army found the Czech tanks to be more durable. As a result, in 1947, Peru attempted to buy 20 upgraded LTP tanks of welded construction, with a Tatra diesel engine, and the more powerful A-7 gun. The contract negotiations dragged on and were finally cancelled by the Communist government in 1951, which complained that Peru had become "a vassal of American imperialism." A small number remained in Peruvian Army service into the late 1980s and were used in counter-insurgency operations against the Shining Path guerilla movement.

Another European sale materialized in 1937 after German and Swedish firms rebuffed attempts by the Swiss Army to purchase tanks. The initial offer was for a version of the AH-IV, but the Swiss wanted a heavier tank with 24mm armor, a Swiss Saurer diesel engine, and a Swiss 24mm Pak 38 cannon. Eventually, a contract was signed for the delivery of 12 Praga LTL-H (H = Helvetia) tanks to the Swiss Army plus a license production agreement. The first 12 tanks were finally delivered to Switzerland in May 1939 in the midst of the German occupation of the Czech provinces. They were designated as Panzerwagen 39 (Pzw 39) in the Swiss Army. Swiss plans to build more tanks were complicated by the German occupation, and in the event, only an additional 12 tanks were completed in Switzerland using knock-down kits provided by ČKD. These tanks were deployed in tank platoons in the Swiss infantry divisions, with four tanks per platoon (Zug). In later years, the platoons were consolidated into larger companies consisting of two platoons with eight tanks. These three companies were attached to the three light brigades. After World War II, many of the tanks were retired to war reserve, but a company remained in service with the Mot.Gren.Btl.11 through the late 1940s.

 A

EARLY EXPORTS

1: PRAGA TNH, 2nd (AFV) REGIMENT, MECHANIZED BRIGADE, IMPERIAL IRANIAN PAHLAVI ARMY, TEHERAN, 1939

The TNH tanks were delivered to Iran in a medium-gray zinc protective paint. The standard markings were painted at the factory, and included the Pahlavi dynasty's imperial crown emblem on the front and a three-digit Arabic numeral in white on the rear sides – in this case, "350." It would appear that the Iranian Army used conventional marking practices, with the three-digit number indicating company, platoon, and individual vehicle.

2: TANQUE 39 (LTP), PERUVIAN TANK BATTALION, PERU–ECUADOR BORDER WAR, SUMMER 1941

The Peruvian LTP tanks were delivered in a factory export camouflage scheme of sand, brown, and green. Their basic marking was a provincial name in white – in this case, "Tacna." During the 1941 border fighting with Ecuador, they carried tactical markings in the form of geometric shapes, probably distinguishing companies. Some tanks had a stylized national insignia in oval form, as shown in the inset drawing here. After the war, they were repainted in an overall drab green color with less prominent markings.

1

2

TACNA

Czechoslovak Army Requirement

From 1935–37 the Czechoslovak Army acquired 298 LT vz. 35 tanks based on the Škoda Š-II-a design. This tank is better known by its later German designation of PzKpfw 35(t). Rather than compete for the domestic orders, Škoda and ČKD came to a cartel arrangement with both firms sharing in the construction program. However, they continued to compete for the design contracts. In 1938, the Czechoslovak Army decided to increase its tank force, and decided to acquire a new light-tank design rather than extend the production of the LT vz. 35. ČKD offered its TNH-S design, which was based on the previous TNH layout but with a more powerful, license-built Scania-Vabis engine, a modified turret with a bustle, and the improved A7 37mm gun. Following the completion of the prototype in early 1938, the TNH-S underwent a series of trials along with improvements. The prototype was demonstrated to Czechoslovak Army officials in 1938. Its excellent performance led to its selection over a rival Škoda offering, followed by a contract for 150 tanks. The new type was officially accepted for Czechoslovak Army service as the LT vz. 38 on August 31, 1938.

To drive down costs, ČKD received army approval to offer the new design for export even before series production had begun. The first two countries to show interest were Sweden and Britain. The original prototype, designated as the TNH-P, was shipped to Britain in February 1939 for trials by the War Mechanisation Board in Farnborough. Any potential sale was cancelled in June 1939 after the German occupation.

The Munich crisis of 1938 significantly disrupted Czechoslovak Army modernization plans. Following the Munich agreement of September 30, 1938, Germany absorbed Czechoslovakia's western borderlands, the Sudetenland. The original plans had called for the completion of all 150 LT vz. 38 tanks by March 1939, but this was delayed by contract negotiations and other complications. In the event, no LT vz. 38 tanks were received by the Czechoslovak Army. On March 15, 1939, Germany occupied the remainder of the Czech provinces under a nominal "Protectorate of Bohemia and Moravia," and permitted the formation of an independent Slovak Republic. Negotiations over the sale of tanks to Sweden continued, but the German occupation pushed off any action for nearly two years.

INTO GERMAN SERVICE

In May 1939, a German delegation from the Heeres Waffenamt (Army Weapons Department) visited ČKD as part of a German program to assess the future role of the Czech armament industry within the Reich. At the time, ten LT vz. 38 tanks had been completed and were still in the factory yards. The remaining 140 tanks were in various stages of completion. The German officers were quite impressed with the new tanks, especially because of their 37mm armament. At the time, German production of the PzKpfw III tank with a comparable 37mm gun had been continually delayed, and there was a desperate need for tanks with a good antitank armament. The vast majority of German tanks at the time were the PzKpfw I with twin 7.92mm machine guns and the PzKpfw II with a 20mm cannon; neither armament was adequate when fighting against modern tanks. The delegation recommended acceptance of the LT vz. 38 into German service, as well as completion of the remainder of the contract. The LT vz. 38 fell in between the existing PzKpfw II light tank and PzKpfw III, having the firepower of the PzKpfw III, but closer in size and weight to the PzKpfw II. The first batch of Czech tanks were accepted for Wehrmacht service in May 1939 as the LTM 38 (Leichte Tank Munster 38) which was simply a German translation of the Czech name, or as Ltm.38 Protektorat. In unit records, it was usually referred to as the Panzer III(t) due to the similarity of its armament to that of the German medium tank. In January 1940, the standard designation PzKpfw 38(t) was introduced. The ČKD company was taken over by German management and was renamed as BMM (Böhmisch-Mährische Maschinenfabrik AG: Bohemia-Moravia Industrial Plant).

The original production run from the Czechoslovak Army contract was designated as PzKpfw 38(t) 1.Serie, later as Ausführung A (Version A). Some modest changes were introduced during the production run, including the addition of a smoke-grenade rack above the exhaust muffler beginning in July 1939. The Notek night-driving light system was introduced towards the end of this series. The final batch of 1.Serie was completed in November 1939.

Combat Debut

The Czechoslovak tanks were primarily used in the mechanization of German cavalry. When World War II started in Europe on September 1, 1939, a total of 78 PzKpfw III(t) tanks had been delivered, enough to equip a single regiment. They were assigned to Panzer-Abteilung.67, the tank

The early versions of the PzKpfw 38(t) had the rear exhaust muffler in a lower position than on subsequent production series. This is a column from the 7.Panzer-Division on the road to Vyazma on October 21, 1941.

A PzKpfw 38(t) Ausf. A Panzerbefelswagen in the SdKfz.268 configuration with the second (rear) radio antenna for the FuG 7 FM radio transceiver and the usual front antenna for the normal Fu 5 tank set. There were two of these radio tanks in each panzer regiment for communicating with Luftwaffe aircraft.

element of the new 3.leichte-Division. The "light" divisions were the name for the German mechanized-cavalry divisions. Panzer-Abteilung.67 had been raised at the garrison at Groß-Glienicke in November 1938 under the command of Oberstleutnant Paul Goerbig. It had gradually been equipped with the PzKpfw III(t) as they became available in June and July 1939. The regiment received 57 tanks prior to the start of the Polish campaign, 55 of these being the standard tank and two PzKpfw III(t) als Bef.Wg. command tanks. The regiment was organized into four companies, and since not enough PzKpfw III(t) were available yet, each company had one platoon (Zug) with PzKpfw II, and two with the PzKpfw III(t). The division saw combat with Heeresgruppe Süd on the southern front in Poland, including the Bzura River battles. Total losses were six or seven tanks, with many others damaged. The knocked-out tanks were later rebuilt.

The Polish campaign made it clear that the armor of the PzKpfw III(t) was inadequate. The Polish Army had been amply equipped with 7.9mm wz.35 antitank rifles and the 37mm wz.36 antitank gun. The antitank rifle could penetrate the frontal armor of the tank at ranges of about 100m, and could penetrate the sides at ranges of 300m. The Polish 37mm antitank gun, a license-produced version of the Swedish Bofors design, could penetrate the PzKpfw III(t) at normal combat ranges. Various 75mm field guns were also used in an antitank role and also were effective against the relatively thin armor of the PzKpfw III(t). This protective weakness was not unique to the Czech design, and was a common problem with all of the German tanks of this era. This resulted in a variety of schemes to improve the tank's frontal armor.

From an organizational standpoint, the army judged the performance of the panzer divisions to have been superior to that of the light-cavalry divisions. As a result, the cavalry's four light divisions were rebuilt as panzer divisions prior to the 1940 campaigns.

A Panzerbefelswagen 38(t) Ausf. C in the SdKfz 267 configuration with a fixed rear frame antenna for the Fu 8 radio transceiver. Two of these served in each panzer regimental headquarters and five more in the divisional armored radio company.

Early Revisions

Although the Waffenamt was not especially enthusiastic about accepting foreign designs, the Czech industrial capacity was an attractive short cut to quickly build up the panzer force. In July 1939, BMM received a second production contract for 325 PzKpfw 38(t) tanks. The intention was to modify the design with more German sub-components. This included the substitution of German radios at the factory, and some German-supplied accessories. The first batch of 110 tanks entered production in January 1940, and these were designated as 2.Serie or Ausf. B. This contract was issued prior to the Polish campaign, and so the armor level remained the same. With the adoption of German radios, the prominent insulated tube on the left side for the old Czechoslovak radios was removed. Tool stowage was standardized on the fenders following the usual German practices. The periscopic sight for the commander had an armored cover added, and a sheet-metal rain gutter was added over the gun-sight aperture. The wheels were modified with a wider rubber tire.

The next batch of 110 Ausf. C (3.Serie) was manufactured from May to August 1940. The first batch of tanks was essentially similar to the Ausf. B due to delays in introducing intended improvements. The most significant technical improvement was the increase in armor based on the lessons of the Polish campaign. The frontal hull armor was increased from 25mm to 40mm, although some of the first tanks in this batch still had the thinner armor. A splashguard was added on the front hull roof to shield the joint between the turret and hull.

TECHNICAL DESCRIPTION

The PzKpfw 38(t) used a conventional configuration, with the fighting compartment in the front and the engine in the rear. There were four crew members, consisting of a tank commander/gunner in the right side of the turret, the loader in the right side of the turret, the bow machine gunner/radio operator on the left side of the hull front, and the driver on the left side. The turret crew had bicycle seats suspended for the turret race (the circular base on

which the turret rests). The two-man turret crew was smaller than the three-man crew preferred in German medium tanks, which meant that the commander had to double up as gunner. Unlike early German light tanks, the PzKpfw 38(t) had a vision cupola for the commander with protected episcopes. The fighting compartment was very cramped and did not provide adequate room for normal crew stowage. As a result, most PzKpfw 38(t) eventually had additional stowage bins fitted externally. These were not included on the tanks when manufactured at BMM, but followed several distinctive patterns. This suggests they were added by the depots such as the main Vienna depot, prior to being issued to troops.

The main gun was a Škoda A7 37mm (L/48) gun, designated as the KwK 38(t) by the Germans. This fired a 37mm round with better antiarmor performance than the German 37mm gun: it had 35mm armor penetration at 500m rather than 29mm. The basic round was the 37mm Pzgr.Patr.37(t) armor-piercing round, which was followed by the improved 37mm Pzgr.Patr.37(t) umg., which added a tracer. A third antitank round, the 37mm Pzgr.40/37(t), was introduced in March 1941 with a tungsten-carbide core, but it was available in smaller quantities due to the shortage of tungsten. The two machine guns were 7.9mm ZB vz. 37, called MG 37(t) by the Germans. The turret machine gun was in a separate ball mount, so could be employed separately from the main gun by the loader, or locked to the main gun for use as a co-axial weapon. Ammunition stowage was 90 rounds of 37mm and 2,700 rounds of 7.92mm machine-gun ammunition.

This illustration of the turret interior from the manual shows: (1) the commander's hatch, (2) the cupola left-side episcope, (3) the cupola front episcope, (4) the turret traverse mechanism, (5) the turret race, (6) the commander's periscopic sight, (7) the commander's TZF.38(t) telescopic gun sight, (8) the gun elevation wheel, (9) the telescopic sight for the co-axial machine gun.

37mm KwK 38(t) gun antitank performance*

Range (m)	37mm Pzgr.Patr.37(t) umg.	37mm Pzgr.40/37(t)
100	40.5	64.0
200	39.0	53.0
400	36.2	38.0
500	34.8	–
1000	28.7	–
1500	24.0	–
*Armor penetration in mm at 30 degrees		

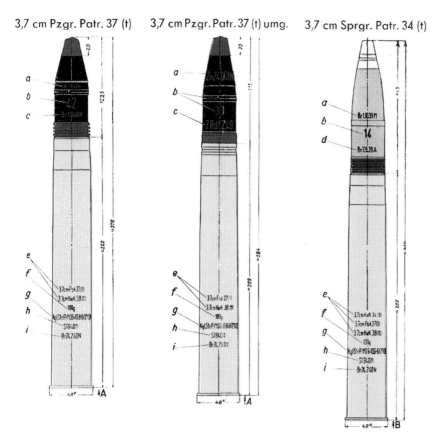

3,7 cm Pzgr. Patr. 37 (t)   3,7 cm Pzgr. Patr. 37 (t) umg.   3,7 cm Sprgr. Patr. 34 (t)

This illustration from the Wehrmacht manual shows the three principal ammunition types for the PzKpfw 38(t). On the left is the 37mm Pzgr. Patr.37(t) armor-piercing round, in the center is the improved 37mm Pzgr.Patr.37(t) umg., and on the right is the 37mm Sprgr. high-explosive round.

The basic tank was fitted with the Fu 2 radio receiver, while platoon commanders had a Fu 5 transmitter as well, requiring the removal of the hull machine gun in order to provide sufficient space in the hull. The radios were mounted in one or two frames on the top of the drive-shaft tunnel between the driver and radio operator.

This interior view of the hull from the technical manual shows the bow gunner/radio operator's station on the left and the driver's station on the right.

A PzKpfw 38(t) Ausf. B of 5. Kompanie, Panzer-Regiment.25, 7.Panzer-Division in Abbeville on June 4, 1940, with an abandoned French 25mm antitank gun behind it.

The engine was a Praga Typ TNHS/II six-cylinder 125hp (92 kW) gasoline engine. The transmission in the front of the vehicle was a Praga-Wilson Typ CV. The power train offered a top road speed of 42km/h (26mph). The tank had a range of about 220km (135 miles).

PzKpfw 38(t) Variants

Ausf.	Serie	Chassis Number	Production	Total
A	1	1–150	May–Nov 1939	150
B	2	151–260	Jan–May 1940	110
C	3	261–370	May–Aug 1940	110
D	4	371–475	Sep–Nov 1940	105
E	5	476–750	Nov 1940–May 1941	275
F	6	751–1000	May–Oct 1941	250
S	n/a	1001–1090	May–Sep 1941	90
G	7	1101–1359; 1480–1526	Oct 1941–Jun 1942	316

GLORY DAYS IN FRANCE

By the time of the 1940 campaign in Western Europe, over 200 PzKpfw 38(t) tanks had been delivered. The absorption of the Czech tanks substantially improved the Wehrmacht's tank-fighting capability in 1940. The Czech tanks amounted to about 13 percent of German tank strength, but accounted for about half of the tanks armed with a 37mm gun. The light tanks such as the PzKpfw I and PzKpfw II were armed with machine guns or 20mm guns that had poor antiarmor power when dealing with the typical French tanks of the period such as the Renault R35 or Hotchkiss H39; the PzKpfw IV had a short 75mm gun designed for high-explosive fire support, not tank fighting.

In 1940, two of the German light mechanized cavalry divisions were rebuilt as panzer divisions with the PzKpfw 38(t) as their principal tank. The 2.leichte-Division became the 7.Panzer-Division and the 3.leichte-Division became 8.Panzer-Division. To strengthen these divisions, two independent

During the autumn of 1940, the 7.Panzer-Division was assigned to take part in the Operation *Sea Lion* invasion of Britain. This PzKpfw 38(t) Ausf. B of 2. Kompanie, Panzer-Regiment.25, 7.Panzer-Division was photographed during a field exercise in the Loire valley near Blevy, France, on November 22, 1940, with a machine-gunner armed with an MG 34 in the foreground.

regiments that had served as army reserve in Poland were added to the light-cavalry divisions in order to bring them up to strength. At the same time, these regiments were re-equipped with the PzKpfw 38(t) tank. This included Panzer-Regiment.25, which went to the new 7.Panzer Division, and Panzer-Regiment.10, which went to the 8.Panzer Division. Overall PzKpfw 38(t) strength on May 10, 1940, was 91 PzKpfw 38(t) and eight PzBef.38(t) in 7.Panzer-Division, and 116 PzKpfw 38(t) and 15 PzBef 38(t) in 8.Panzer Division. Due to continuing shortages of PzKpfw 38(t), both divisions were fleshed out with older PzKpfw I and PzKpfw II light tanks. In addition, their medium companies were equipped with the new PzKpfw IV tanks.

Erwin Rommel's 7.Panzer-Division is no doubt the more famous of the two divisions equipped with the PzKpfw 38(t) in France. It was dubbed the "Ghost Division" (*Gespensterdivision*) after its exploits in France. The division served with 4.Armee, part of Heeresgruppe A, which executed the "Sickle cut" through the Ardennes. This was not part of the Gruppe Kleist armored spearhead, but served on its right flank. The PzKpfw 38(t) proved well suited to Rommel's tactics. Instead of directly confronting the French armored force, Rommel exploited his division's mobility by using a modern version of the classic infiltration tactics of 1918. Having penetrated the Belgian border defenses, Rommel's tanks pushed down the Morville–Flavion road towards an inevitable confrontation with the French 1e Division Cuirasée. The French armored divisions were substantially smaller than those of their German opponents, but they were equipped with the powerful Char B1 bis tank and the well-armored Hotchkiss H39 infantry tank. On May 15, 1940, Oberst Rothenburg's Panzer-Regiment.25 was confronted by a Char B1 bis company of the 28e BCC (tank battalion) outside Flavion. Five German tanks were hit in quick succession. Rommel's eye was not on a pitched tank battle, and so he dispatched his divisional Flak batteries with 88mm guns to keep the Char B1 bis tanks at bay while his division continued westward. During the advance later in the morning, Rommel's forces caught the rest of the 28e BCC (Char B1 bis) and 25e BCC (H39) when they were vulnerable during their refueling, and disrupted them, but kept moving forward. He left it up to the neighboring 5.Panzer-Division to deal with the remaining threat of the 1e DCR.

By May 19, 7.Panzer-Division was in the vanguard of 4.Armee and reached the Cambrai area. This placed it in the middle of the tank battles with French and British units around Arras during the second week of the campaign. Once again, Rommel refrained from pitting his thinly armored vehicles against the Allied tanks, and the division's infantry and 88mm guns bore the brunt of the Allied tank attacks. The 7.Panzer-Division remained on the western side of the Dunkirk pocket until early June 1940. The PzKpfw 38(t) proved well suited to a campaign of rapid movement, but it was not ideal for tank-vs-tank combat. Its 37mm gun was poorly suited to fighting against the thickly armored French tanks, which were nearly impervious

B

EARLY BLITZKRIEG OPERATIONS

1: PzKpfw 38(t) AUSF. A, 3./PANZER-ABTEILUNG.67, 3.LEICHTE-DIVISION, POLISH CAMPAIGN, SEPTEMBER 1939

Since June 1937, German tanks were finished in overall RAL 46 Dunklegrau (dark gray) with patches of RAL 45 Dunklebraun (dark brown) spray painted on about a third of the surface. This replaced the earlier Reichswehr Buntfarbenanstrich multi-color camouflage scheme.

At the time of the Polish campaign, the Wehrmacht used a plain cross as national insignia, as seen here. This insignia proved too visible to enemy antitank gunners, and was abandoned after the campaign, being replaced with a reduced-visibility style. For air identification, a white rectangle about 90cm wide and 50cm high was painted on the engine deck.

In the 1930s, tactical numbers were painted in white on a black, detachable plate carried on either side of the vehicle. The plate was rhomboid in shape, mimicking the standard Wehrmacht map symbol for tanks. Panzer-Abteilung.67 also had a painted rhomboid on the lower rear turret side. The precise pattern is unknown, but probably followed the army practice based on the traditional bayonet knot colors. Sub-formations used different colors depending on their sequence: 1 (white); 2 (red); 3 (yellow); 4 (blue); 5 (light green); HQ and staff (dark green). In the case of Pz.Abt.67, the rhomboid was often edged in white.

2: BEFELSPANZER 38(t) (SD.KFZ.267), 2.PANZER-FUNKKOMPANIE, NACHRICHTEN-ABTEILUNG.83, 7.PANZER-DIVISION, FRANCE, MAY 1940

At the time of the battle of France in May–June 1940, German tanks were still officially in the two-color gray/brown camouflage scheme as seen here. Tactical markings began to change as a result of the lessons learned in the 1939 Polish campaign. The solid white cross was dropped in favor of a less conspicuous "hollow" cross with the center either left in the dark base colors of the vehicle or painted black.

The rhomboid tactical number still remained in use, but was too small to be useful in combat conditions. As a result, some units began to paint much more conspicuous tactical numbers on the turret side. For most tanks the pattern was a three-digit number indicating company/platoon/tank. In the case of command vehicles, the regimental HQ/staff would use an "R" prefix such as "R01." The Abteilung headquarters within a regiment would sometimes use a "I" prefix for the first and a "II" for the second battalion, such as "I01, II01." Use of other lettered prefixes for specialized sub-formations was idiosyncratic to each division. The 7.Panzer-Division used especially prominent numbers. The color patterns for these numbers is not certain, but may have been based on the traditional bayonet-knot scheme.

Tactical map symbols were sometimes used on vehicles, in this case the armored radio company of the divisional signals battalion, which was carried on the lower bow (as shown in the inset drawing) and on the right rear hull. This company had the heaviest concentration of radio tanks, nominally five *Befelspanzer* in the Sd.Kfz.267 configuration. By the time of the battle of France, the use of small divisional insignia had become standard, in this case the inverted "Y" with three dots for 7.Panzer-Division carried on the lower bow and hull rear. The use of a large white rectangle on the engine deck for air recognition remained in place since the 1939 fighting.

from the front. Rommel's tactics made best use of the PzKpfw 38(t)'s mobility while minimizing its inadequate firepower and armor. The successes of the "Ghost Division" were won more often by boldness and mobility than either firepower or armored protection.

Following the evacuation of the British Expeditionary Force from Dunkirk, 7.Panzer-Division took part in the push southward past Rouen, again spearheading the 4.Armee and executing the breakthrough to the Seine River. It reached Fécamp on the Channel coast on June 10. During the third week of June, it took part in the push through lower Normandy, eventually taking part in the capture of Cherbourg on June 20. It claimed about 460 French tanks and armored cars destroyed or captured, and took more than 97,000 Allied prisoners. Its exemplary performance came at a price. The division suffered higher casualties in France than any other German division. Its vehicle losses included 42 tanks, of which 26 were PzKpfw 38(t).

The 8.Panzer-Division, led by Gen.Lt. Adolf Kuntzen, remained in the shadows of the more famous 7.Panzer-Division in France. It served in Gen. Maj. Werner Kempf's XXXI.Korps, part of the Gruppe von Kleist panzer concentration that burst out of the Ardennes. As it happened, the division was in the second echelon during the initial assault into France. It took part in the race to the Channel during the third week of May 1940, establishing the northwest boundary of the Dunkirk pocket, but it did not play a central role in the attack.

A total of 54 PzKpfw 38(t) tanks were written off after the French campaign, but all but six were later rebuilt at BMM.

A classic image of a PzKpfw 38(t) Ausf. E of Panzer-Regiment.25, 7.Panzer-Division on the first day of Operation *Barbarossa* on June 22, 1941, when the unit was pushing through Lithuania near the town of Kalvariya.

LATE-PRODUCTION VERSIONS

Production of the PzKpfw 38(t) continued, in spite of its modest firepower and armor. German intelligence on its future adversary, the Red Army, was not especially good. The overall impression was that the Soviet tank force relied primarily on types such as the T-26 and BT-7, which were similar in firepower and armor to the PzKpfw 38(t). The encounters with the heavily armored French and British tanks in the summer of 1940 were ignored in favor of rapidly building up the panzer force. In view of Russia's enormous geographic boundaries, the Wehrmacht planned to employ double the number of panzer divisions by the summer of 1941. Czech production was vital to this goal. The final batch of 105 Ausf. D (4.Serie) was essentially similar to the Ausf. C, though small detail changes were introduced during production. The Czech antenna pot was finally eliminated in favor of the standard German antenna mount. A new pattern of track was introduced. Small detail changes were made to the front hull plate.

By early 1940, the PzKpfw 38(t) had seen its combat debut in Poland, and crew comments were favorable enough that a new contract was awarded to BMM for 250 more tanks. The main technical innovation in this Ausf. E batch was to increase the frontal armor to offer better protection against enemy antitank guns. Production took place from November 1940 to May 1941. The turret front was improved by adding a 25mm face-hardened plate

over the existing 25mm plate, offering a total of 50mm of protection. Turret side armor was increased to 30mm, and to 25mm on the turret rear. The upper hull sides received an additional 15mm of armor. The upper front hull on previously produced tanks had been curved, and to rationalize the design for the armor increase this plate was changed to a simple flat plate. To accommodate the extra ton of weight, an additional leaf spring was added to the suspension. A revised rear exhaust muffler was introduced with a smoke-grenade rack in an armored cover. The next series of Ausf. F was essentially similar to the Ausf. E, with very minor production differences. The number of rivets on the engine deck was reduced, the spare-track stowage on the right rear fender was increased from two to three links, and some of the final tanks had the front Notek light moved to the left front corner of the glacis plate.

The PzKpfw 38(t) Ausf. F continued the process of reducing the external rivets in the hull construction, most noticeably on the lower lip of the rear engine doors.

In 1940–41, the German firm Kassböhrer developed the AP-1 floatation system for the PzKpfw 38(t) for use in river crossing or amphibious operations, with plans to manufacture 100 sets. In the event, the program did not progress beyond trials in the Vltava River.

PzKpfw 38(t) AUSF. E

Technical data	
Crew	four (commander/gunner, loader, driver, radioman)
Weight	9.8 metric tonnes (21,700lb)
Length	4.61m (15.1ft)
Width	2.135m (7ft)
Height	2.252m (7.4ft)
Main armament	37mm KwK 38(t) gun
Elevation	-10 +25 degrees
Sight	TzF 38(t), 2.6x, 25-degree field of view
Secondary armament	two x 7.92mm MG 37(t); one machine gun on platoon command tanks
Ammunition	90 rounds of 37mm, 2,700 rounds of 7.92mm
Communications	Fu 5 and Fu 2 transceiver (platoon commander)
Engine	Praga Typ TNHPS/II 125hp, six-cylinder gasoline engine
Transmission	Praga-Wilson Typ CV, one reverse gear, five forward gears
Steering	clutch-brake
Fuel	220 liters (58gal)
Range	100km cross country, 250km road (60–155 miles)
Maximum speed	42km/h (26mph)
Power-to-weight ratio	12.7hp/ton
Ground pressure	0.64kg/cm^2

KEY

1. Engine muffler
2. Praga Typ TNHPS/II engine
3. Tank commander's seat
4. Gun breech safety frame
5. Tank commander's vision cupola
6. Tank commander's rotating periscopic sight
7. Breech of 37mm KwK 38(t) gun
8. Co-axial 7.92mm MG 37(t) machine gun
9. Radio antenna
10. 7.92mm MG 37(t) machine gun
11. Notek night driving light
12. Drive sprocket
13. Praga-Wilson Typ CV transmission
14. Bogie spring suspension unit
15. Fu 2 radio receiver
16. Loader's seat
17. Road-wheel
18. Idler wheel

THE SWEDISH DIVERSION

Sweden had already acquired the AH-IV tankettes, and in early 1939 expressed interest in a more modern light tank. In March 1939, ČKD made an offer to sell 50 TNH-Sv tanks, but with the German occupation a few days later, this deal fell through. Since Germany was obtaining nickel-and-ball bearings from Sweden for its own war industries, there were no immediate objections when the Swedish government attempted to revive the sales later in 1939. A contract was signed between the new BMM management and Sweden in March 1940 for the delivery of 90 tanks, the first 15 tanks in June 1940 and the final batch by October 1940. Manufacture of these tanks was begun in June 1940, but on July 18, 1940, the OKH (Oberkommando des Heeres: Army High Command) confiscated the entire lot of equipment, including ball bearings and raw material provided from Sweden. These 90 Swedish tanks were absorbed by the Wehrmacht as the PzKpfw 38(t) Ausf. S. They were something of a hybrid in regards to many of the small production details, since the TNH-Sv had been designed prior to the Ausf. F, but production had taken place alongside the Ausf. F. In terms of armor, it had the upgrades to the turret and hull front but not the turret or hull sides. There were many other small differences of detail as a result.

BATTLES ON THE RUSSIAN FRONT

The PzKpfw 38(t) again saw combat in Operation *Marita*, the invasion of Yugoslavia, starting on April 6, 1940. During the brief fighting there, the 8.Panzer-Division recorded a total loss of seven PzKpfw 38(t). The PzKpfw 38(t) proved to be a durable vehicle in the mountains, and kept running even after many other German tanks had broken down.

At the time of Operation *Barbarossa* in June 1941, the PzKpfw 38(t) equipped five of the 17 panzer divisions taking part in the invasion of the

Invasion day, June 22, 1941. This is a view of a column from Panzer-Regiment.25, 7.Panzer-Division south of Kalvariya, Lithuania, led by a PzKpfw 38(t) Ausf. C. This is a *Zugführerwagen* (platoon leader's vehicle) with the hull machine gun removed and its opening plated over in order to accommodate the extra radio set.

Soviet Union. As in France, they were deployed in place of the PzKpfw III. The PzKpfw 38(t) represented about 14 percent of total panzer inventory, but amounted to 20 percent of the tanks actually taking part in the attack since the obsolete PzKpfw I was being gradually eased out of service. The PzKpfw 38(t) was comparable or superior to the vast bulk of the Soviet tank force, which was made up primarily of the T-26 light tank and BT-7 cavalry tank. The PzKpfw 38(t) had comparable gun performance to its main Soviet adversaries, and better frontal armor in its later versions. Soviet tanks typically were limited to about 15mm of armor, while the later versions of the PzKpfw 38(t) had 50mm of frontal armor. One of the main technical advantages enjoyed by the PzKpfw 38(t) was that it was more durable than its Soviet counterparts, which had a low life expectancy, exacerbated by a shortage of spare parts. The PzKpfw 38(t) was completely outmatched by the Soviet T-34 and KV tanks, though these types were rarely encountered in the summer 1941 fighting.

Tank fighting in summer 1941 was not uncommon, but German tactics emphasized the role of the panzer divisions in exploiting breakthroughs to encircle the much larger Soviet forces. Combat as often as not involved confrontations with Soviet rifle divisions. The standard Soviet 45mm antitank gun could penetrate the frontal armor of the PzKpfw 38(t) at short combat ranges. Although the new Soviet 14.5mm antitank rifles had begun to appear in Soviet service, they were not yet the menace they would prove to be in later years of the campaign. The PzKpfw 38(t) had battlefield survivability nearly identical to the PzKpfw III and PzKpfw IV tanks, with the five panzer divisions suffering about 27 percent losses in their PzKpfw 38(t) tanks in June–August 1941. Mines were a particular problem, and the 20.Panzer-Division estimated that half of their combat losses of the PzKpfw 38(t) were due to mines. Due to its smaller size, encounters with mines usually resulted in heavier casualties among drivers and radio operators in the front of the tank compared with larger and heavier tanks such as the PzKpfw IV.

One of the main technical problems facing German tank units in Russia was the sheer distance involved in the advance. Tanks of this era did not have

This captured Soviet PzKpfw 38(t) Ausf. S was part of a trainload of ten of these tanks being shipped from repair factories in the Moscow area to Maj. Nebylov's Separate Tank Battalion of the 20th Army on the Western Front in July 1942.

especially great range, and their durability was badly affected by long road marches in dusty conditions, which degraded engine durability. By late August and early September 1941, the five panzer divisions employing the PzKpfw 38(t) only had about 58 percent of their tanks fit for action, with the rest in repair. This level of durability of the PzKpfw 38(t) was similar to that of the PzKpfw IV, and somewhat better than the PzKpfw III, which continued to suffer from transmission problems.

Durability and losses of German tank types, Aug–Sep 1941

(Percentage)	PzKpfw II	PzKpfw III	PzKpfw IV	PzKpfw 38
Operational	73	48	58	58
In Repair	27	52	42	42
Losses	19	28	27	27

The PzKpfw 38(t) suffered from the same problems afflicting other German tanks in the autumn and winter of 1941–42. Its narrow tracks were not ideal in the muddy autumn conditions on Russia's poor roads. Its performance in the cold winter months was poor, due both to its poor floatation in snow and its poor engine performance in extreme cold. Losses from mechanical problems rose alarmingly in the winter of 1941–42. Total PzKpfw 38(t) losses in 1941 were over 800 tanks out of a starting strength of fewer than 700 at the beginning of Operation *Barbarossa*. In the case of the 7.Panzer-Division, of its 151 losses in 1941, 99 were due to enemy action and 52 tanks were abandoned due to mechanical breakdown. The 20. Panzer-Division, which was one of the units to reach the outskirts of Moscow in December 1941, reported on the problems of operating the PzKpfw 38(t) in the winter conditions:

> Icy roads significantly lengthened travel times on roads with vehicle without cleats. Small hills and slopes decreased speed even if cleats could be attached. Rapid movement in combat was greatly hindered… It was necessary to start the vehicles at least every two hours, which disturbed the troops' sleep and increased fuel consumption. Thinner oil was needed in low temperatures. Attack in snowstorms or even in powdery snow obstructed vision from gun sights and vision ports… Turrets must be traversed now and then to prevent them from freezing tight… A large number of panzers were stuck in snow

D **PzKpfw 38(t) AUSF. F, II./PANZER-REGIMENT.204, 22.PANZER-DIVISION, CRIMEA, SUMMER 1942**

In June 1940, a general order was issued to stop applying the dark-brown color to armored-vehicle camouflage, leaving the tanks in a uniform dark-gray color, eventually redesignated as RAL 7017. The 22.Panzer-Division was the last division to be fully equipped with the PzKpfw 38(t), so its vehicles were delivered in overall dark gray. The conditions in the Crimea were far more arid than most of Russia, and the dark-gray color was not ideal camouflage. As a result, many of the division's tanks were given a hasty camouflage scheme prior to the summer fighting in the Crimea. Since German tank units were not regularly issued camouflage paint at this stage of the war, the scheme was either improvised using local resources, or applied using mud. The latter seems more likely here, given the sloppy finish.

By this stage of World War II, the use of three-digit tactical numbers had become commonplace, though the particular style varied from division to division. In the case of some companies in II./PzAbt.204, notably 5./Pz.Rgt.204, a white line was painted under the number. The significance of this marking is not clear.

over 20cm deep because the depth of drifts and depressions is not clear. Repairs in cold temperatures and snow are extremely difficult. On hard frozen and packed trails, broken springs and all types of suspension damage occur.

Some of the PzKpfw 38(t) tanks that were abandoned during the hard winter of 1941–42 due to mechanical breakdowns subsequently were recovered by the Red Army. They were rebuilt in several factories, most notably the Moscow MZOK VIM plant (Mashinostroitelniy zavod opytnykh mekhanizatsiya selskogo khozyastva: Experimental Industrial Plant for the Mechanization of the Rural Economy). The MG.37 machine gun was often replaced by the Soviet DT machine gun to simplify ammunition supply. Most of the tanks repaired in Moscow were sent to the nearby Zapadniy Front (Western Front). At least two independent tank battalions were formed there in the summer of 1942 using captured German tanks: the Nebylov Battalion with the 20th Army and "Letter B" battalion with the 31st Army. Major Nebylov's battalion had ten PzKpfw 38(t) along with 12 PzKpfw III, six PzKpfw IV, and two StuG III. This unit remained in combat through October 1942, by which time it had lost most of its captured tanks. The total number of PzKpfw 38(t) used by the Red Army is not known, but probably totaled a few dozen. By late 1942, supplies of Czech 37mm gun ammunition became so difficult to find that some surviving PzKpfw 38(t) tanks had Soviet 45mm tank guns substituted. There was a scheme in 1944 to rebuild remaining tanks as the SAU ZIS-57 tank destroyer with the ZIS-2 57mm antitank at Zavod No. 92 in Gorkiy, but it is unclear how many, if any, were converted.

FINAL PzKpfw 38(t) PRODUCTION TYPES

The PzKpfw 38(t) had proven to be a durable and dependable design and so in late 1941, further production contracts were awarded to BMM. The plan was to ramp up production to 65 per month through October 1942, at which point there would be a short interlude until April 1943 when the "New Variant" PzKpfw 38(t) would enter production. The new contract batch of PzKpfw 38(t) Ausf. G was very similar to the final production series of Ausf. F. One of the main efforts was to simplify production. As a result, the armor shifted from sandwiched, face-hardened armor to new homogenous 50mm plate armor on the turret, superstructure, and hull front. Other small changes were made too, including a reduction in the number of rivets on various locations.

By early 1942, it was becoming obvious that tanks armed with 37mm guns were completely inadequate for operations on the Russian front due to the increasing prevalence of T-34 and KV tanks. More firepower was needed, but the PzKpfw 38(t) had too small a turret ring to accommodate a 50mm gun. There was no simple way to increase the turret-ring diameter sufficiently short of completely redesigning the tank. Furthermore, by this stage of the war, the Wehrmacht preferred three-man turrets, not the two-man turret of the PzKpfw 38(t), which overworked the commander. Work was already underway to convert obsolete PzKpfw I tanks into *Panzerjäger* (tank destroyer) configurations by mounting a large antitank gun in an open casemate. In January 1942, the Waffenamt decided to cease production

A PzKpfw 38(t) Ausf. G in the BMM factory yard in June 1942. By this stage of production, the Notek light had been moved from the mud guard to the right front corner of the glacis plate.

of PzKpfw 38(t) tanks in favor of using the chassis for tank destroyers. Of the Ausf. G (7.Serie), 306 were built as light tanks and the remainder as tank destroyers of the Marder III family. The BMM production lines in May–June 1942 produced both types, and the last PzKpfw 38(t), chassis number 1526, left the factory on June 20, 1942. The total number of PzKpfw 38(t) tanks was 1,396, plus 37 for the Slovak Army.

German PzKpfw 38(t) deployment and losses

1939	Jan	Feb	Mar	Apr	May	June	July	Aug	Sept	Oct	Nov	Dec	Total
Strength						9	21	60	78	103	141	144	
Losses									6				6
1940	**Jan**	**Feb**	**Mar**	**Apr**	**May**	**June**	**July**	**Aug**	**Sept**	**Oct**	**Nov**	**Dec**	**Total**
Strength	144	154	178	209	238	233	253	277	320	357	401	432	
Losses					43	11							54
1941	**Jan**	**Feb**	**Mar**	**Apr**	**May**	**June**	**July**	**Aug**	**Sept**	**Oct**	**Nov**	**Dec**	**Total**
Strength	476	520	570	636	686	754	763	661	543	547	528	434	
Losses					7	33	182	183	82	85	149	102	823
1942	**Jan**	**Feb**	**Mar**	**Apr**	**May**	**June**	**July**	**Aug**	**Sept**	**Oct**	**Nov**	**Dec**	**Total**
Strength	381	424	491	522	521	454	479	479	436	375	334	309	
Losses	21	8	13	22	6	4	5	20	24	37	25	18	203
1943	**Jan**	**Feb**	**Mar**	**Apr**	**May**	**June**	**July**	**Aug**	**Sept**	**Oct**	**Nov**	**Dec**	**Total**
Strength	287	252	242	161	186	197	204	212	201	255	260	249	
Losses	30	12	30	4	2			1	1	5	10	1	96
1944	**Jan**	**Feb**	**Mar**	**Apr**	**May**	**June**	**July**	**Aug**	**Sept**	**Oct**	**Nov**	**Dec**	**Total**
Strength	227	227	227	227	229	232	229	229	140	138	136		

*Loss figures for 1944 not available

A rear view of a PzKpfw 38(t) in the BMM yard in May 1942 showing the features of the final production batch.

THE DECLINE OF THE PzKpfw 38(t)

Because of the decision to end PzKpfw 38(t) production, the Wehrmacht had to decide about the fate of the five panzer divisions still equipped with this type. At the beginning of 1942, there were only 381 PzKpfw 38(t) operational on the Russian front due to the heavy losses in the hard winter of 1941–42. Further complicating this issue was the work underway to field the new 22.Panzer-Division with the PzKpfw 38(t) as well as a plan to reinforce the Hungarian Army with 100 PzKpfw 38(t). After studying several alternatives, Berlin decided to let the panzer divisions located in Heeresgruppe Nord and Mitte (Army Group North and Center) to atrophy, with their PzKpfw 38(t) inventory declining from regimental to battalion strength. Instead, the units assigned to Heeresgruppe Süd would be given preference for replacements since the plans for the summer campaign envisioned this sector as being the focus of operations for the Ostheer (Eastern Army). *Fall Blau* (Plan Blue) was intended to push towards the Don River and to seize the Soviet oilfields in the Caucasus.

In the event, 7.Panzer-Division was shipped back to Western Europe for reconstruction in early 1942 and left its PzKpfw 38(t) behind with 1.Panzer-Division and 2.Panzer-Division. These were deployed in small *Kampfgruppen* (battle groups), which gradually evaporated due to combat attrition through 1942. The 1.Panzer-Division concentrated the PzKpfw 38(t) in Kampfgruppe Koll and found them to be of declining value as more and more T-34 tanks appeared on the battlefield. They reported in April 1942 that "These Panzers are knocked out by the T-34 at ranges of 200 to 800m. The Panzer 38(t) can't destroy or repulse a T-34 at these ranges. Because of its gun, a T-34 can knock out an attacking panzer at long range."

The 12.Panzer-Division was converted to the PzKpfw III in 1942, and so this left only three divisions (8., 19., and 20.) on the Russian front with the dwindling number of PzKpfw 38(t) through the spring and summer 1942 campaigns.

Swansong of the PzKpfw 38(t): *Fall Blau*

The largest concentration of PzKpfw 38(t) tanks in the campaigns in the spring and summer of 1942 belonged to Panzer-Regiment.204 of the 22. Panzer-Division. This unit was formed in France in 1941 and saw its combat debut in southern Russia in March 1942. When initially arriving in Russia, it had only two of its three tank battalions, with a strength of 77 PzKpfw 38(t) tanks. The 22.Panzer-Division was assigned to Heeresgruppe Süd in anticipation of the *Fall Blau* campaign to capture the Caucasus oil fields. The hardened veterans of the 1941–42 winter campaigns derisively labeled the new unit as the "Eau-de-Cologne Division" because it "arrived from the West and evaporated quickly." Like many inexperienced units, the division mistakenly believed that the Red Army units could easily be overwhelmed by a brisk tank attack.

The division's combat debut on March 20, 1942, near Novo-Mikhailovka on the Kerch peninsula in the Crimea, was a debacle. A total of 33 tanks, including 17 PzKpfw 38(t), were destroyed by the Soviet antitank defenses and tank counterattacks, and many more tanks damaged. The division was subsequently pulled back for further training. The III.Abteilung of Panzer-Regiment.204 finally arrived in April, but spent much of the spring and summer campaign detached as Kampfgruppe Rodt. The division received replacements, including some new PzKpfw III tanks, prior to the renewal of the attacks against the heavily defended Kerch peninsula in May 1942.

In early May 1942, the 22.Panzer-Division was committed to *Unternehmen Trappenjagd* (Operation *Bustard Hunt*) against the Soviet Crimean Front guarding the approaches to the Kerch peninsula. The PzKpfw 38(t) still remained a viable tank in this theater, as Red Army tank strength contained large numbers of light tanks and fewer T-34 and KV tanks. Prior to the German offensive on May 8, 1942, Soviet tank strength in the Crimea totaled 178 tanks, of which 139 were T-26 and T-60 light tanks, both of which were vulnerable to the 37mm gun of the PzKpfw 38(t). In contrast to its performance in March 1942, by May the division had learned its lessons and

The 22.Panzer-Division was the last unit to be fully equipped with the PzKpfw 38(t). It was deployed to the Crimea in March 1942, and one from 8.Kompanie, Panzer-Regiment.204 is seen disembarking from a barge on the Black Sea during operations in the summer of 1942.

A PzKpfw 38(t) Ausf. F platoon command tank leads a column from 7./Panzer-Regiment.204 during the fighting in the Crimea in the spring of 1942.

no longer underestimated the Red Army. During the German attack on May 8–9, the 22.Panzer-Division made a deep penetration of Soviet infantry positions, prompting the Crimean Front to commit its 55th Tank Brigade and 229th Separate Tank Battalion to a tank counterattack. In the ensuing tank skirmishes on May 9 against Panzer-Regiment.204, the Soviet tank units took heavy losses. By May 11, the Soviet 55th Tank Brigade had been reduced from 46 to 20 tanks in three days of fighting and the 229th Separate Tank Battalion had all 11 of its KV tanks destroyed or disabled. The attack by the 22.Panzer-Division was instrumental in enveloping the Soviet 47th Army and pinning it against the Sea of Azov. Following its successful use at Kerch, the 22.Panzer-Division was returned to Heeresgruppe Süd for a succession of attacks against the Soviet Southwest Front, starting with Operation *Wilhelm* (June 10–15), Operation *Fredidericus II* (June 22–25), and Operation *Braunschweig* (after June 28). In the third week of July 1942, the division took part in the Don River campaign, advancing to Rostov-na-Don, the gateway to the Caucasus. It was subsequently transferred to Heeresgruppe B where it was used to support the weak Italian 8a Armata ARMIR (Armata Italiana in Russia).

At the end of August 1942, the III./Pz.Rgt.204 was detached permanently from the division to form Gruppe Michalik, the seed of the Panzer-Abteilung.127 for the newly formed 27.Panzer-Division near Voronezh. This badly under-strength formation had barely 26 PzKpfw 38(t), and was used in the fighting along the Don and Donets rivers where it was gradually reduced to a handful of tanks by the late autumn.

Having lost one of its three tank battalions, by the early autumn of 1942 the 22.Panzer-Division had only about half of its starting tank strength, with around 50 PzKpfw 38(t) still in service. It was partly reorganized in October 1942, giving up all but five of its PzKpfw 38(t) to the new Panzer-Verband 700. During the Soviet counteroffensive in November 1942, Operation *Uranus*, the division attempted to prevent the encirclement of the 6.Armee in Stalingrad, but barely escaped the encirclement itself. The commander of Heeresgruppe Don, Erich von Manstein, labeled the division "a complete wreck."

Panzer-Verband.700 was formed at the end of October 1942 and used to reinforce the weak Hungarian 2nd Army on the Stalingrad front. By this stage, its PzKpfw 38(t) tanks from the 22.Panzer-Division were badly worn out, and by the end of November 1942, only 17 of 50 tanks were operational. The unit complained that, "Due to its armor and armament, these panzers can't be used to fight Russian tanks. The Typ 38(t) can only be classified as totally outdated. Also it is mechanically unsuitable for planned employment in arid areas. At temperatures of over 30 degrees Celsius, the engine overheats and stops. To fulfill the assigned objective, the unit must be outfitted with at least the PzKpfw III (lang)." On January 13, 1943, it had 27 PzKpfw 38(t) tanks when it was overwhelmed by the Red Army's *Little Saturn* offensive.

The number of PzKpfw 38(t) tanks in service with the panzer divisions continued to decline through 1943. Those withdrawn from the tank regiments were shifted to reconnaissance battalions to serve as light scout tanks. At the time of the battles around Kursk in the summer of 1943, there were only 13 still in front-line service in Russia, three with the 8.Panzer-Division and nine with the 20.Panzer-Division. However, there were still more than 200 in Wehrmacht inventory. The reason for this discrepancy was that most remaining PzKpfw 38(t) tanks had been withdrawn to other roles. Some had their turrets removed and were used as Munitionsfahrzeug 38(t) to support

LEFT
Some of the old PzKpfw 38(t) were retired from the panzer regiments and used as scout tanks by divisional reconnaissance battalions. This PzKpfw 38(t) Ausf. C of Panzer-Aufklärungs-Abteilung.24, 12.Panzer-Division was lost during the fighting with the Red Army on January 26, 1945, in the East Prussian town of Tolkemit.

RIGHT
When operating with the new BP-42 and BP-44 armored trainers, the PzKpfw 38(t) was deployed from a *Panzerträgerwagen*. This specialized rail car had a folding ramp on the front that allowed the tank to disembark and support the train's infantry detachment. The *Panzerträgerwagen* was lightly armored to protect the tank's suspension. Armored trains were allotted two of these, usually at either end of the train.

A pair of PzKpfw 38(t) Ausf. E of an armored-train detachment, finished in the new 1943 camouflage scheme.

self-propelled artillery units. Other PzKpfw 38(t) tanks were assigned to various small *Panzer-Sicherung Kompanien* (armored security companies) for anti-partisan work in the hinterlands of Belarus, Ukraine, and Poland. They were also assigned to *Panzer-Ersatz-und Ausbildungs-Abteilungen* (tank replacement and training units). On occasion, these training tanks were pressed into combat service in the desperate days of 1944–45, as can be seen on some of the accompanying photos here. The most significant of their new missions was their use by German armored-train units.

Anti-Partisan Tanks

Inspektion.10 of the Wehrmacht's railroad engineer office was responsible for raising and equipping armored-train units (*Eisenbahn-Panzerzüge*). While these units were not especially significant in 1939–41, the invasion of Russia in 1941 created the need for a larger number of more sophisticated armored trains to protect the railroad lines from Soviet partisans. The Wehrmacht adopted the Polish tactic of assigning tanks to the armored trains. The tanks were useful since they could be dismounted from flat-cars and carry out missions away from the train in support of the train's infantry detachment. At first, the German armored trains used war-booty French tanks including the Somua S35, the Renault FT, and the Hotchkiss H39. By 1942, Inspektion.10 attempted to standardize the configuration of the armored trains. With the PzKpfw 38(t) being withdrawn from front-line service, these became available for use by the railway units. At first, these were deployed from ordinary railroad flat-cars. In 1942, a dedicated rail-car was developed for the PzKpfw 38(t), called the *Panzerträgerwagen*, as part of the program to develop a standardized armored train, the BP-42 (Behelfsmäßiger Panzerzug 1942). The armored trains organized under the BP-42 and the later BP-44 configurations had two of these specialized tank cars, usually positioned on either end of the train. The *Panzerträgerwagen* nestled the PzKpfw 38(t) low in its frame in order to offer better protection, and had folding ramps at the front to make it easier to deploy the tank from the train.

E

PARTISAN WAR IN THE EAST: PzKpfw 38(t) AUSF G, PANZERZUG PZ.62, UKRAINE, 1944

After its retirement from front-line service, the PzKpfw 38(t) was deployed in secondary roles, most notably for tank support of German armored-train regiments. The standard deployment pattern was two tanks per train. At first, the PzKpfw 38(t) were deployed on flat cars. This was not especially efficient, since it was time consuming and awkward to move the tank off the flat car. During the development of the improved BP 42 design, a specialized *Panzerträgerwagen* was developed for the PzKpfw 38(t) that had folding ramps at one end, providing a more efficient method for rapidly deploying the tank to support the train's dismounted infantry detachment (*Schützengruppe*). In this fashion, the armored train became a combined-arms team, with a mobile tank/infantry detachment operating away from the train, while the train itself provided artillery fire support from its artillery cars (*Geschützwagen*).

Many of the tanks assigned to the armored trains were rebuilt prior to being deployed with the trains, and during this process they were repainted in the new 1943 camouflage scheme. This revision from the former overall dark-gray scheme was adopted under the new February 1943 instructions (Heeresmitteilung 1943 Nr. 181). The basic color was overall RAL 7028 Dunkelgelb (dark yellow) with spray-painted patterns of RAL 6003 Olivgrün (olive green) and RAL 8017 Rotbraun (red brown). The tanks assigned to the trains usually had the standard cross painted on the turret side, but they seldom carried tactical numbers. Some of the trains had their own tactical symbol, such as the sunburst insignia used by PZ.62. This insignia was painted on the tank in reduced size, usually on the round plate over the hull machine-gun opening.

Some of the old PzKpfw 38(t) that were retired to training and replacement units were thrown into combat in the desperate final months of World War II. This PzKpfw 38(t) Ausf. A was captured by Patton's Third US Army during the fighting with the 416. Infanterie-Division near Oberperl along the Orscholz–Reigel defense line of the Westwall in the Saarland in late November 1944.

Festung Drehtürm

The decision to prematurely terminate the production of the PzKpfw 38(t) Ausf. G left the BMM plant with about 200 turrets in various states of completion. With the *Atlantikwall* fortification program underway, 225 turrets were transferred from BMM to the fortification engineers in 1942–43 for incorporation into the coastal defenses. These were generally mounted on a modified version of the standard Bauform 67 Ringstand, the Bauform 241. Besides the new-production "*Normalserie*" turrets provided by BMM, turrets from damaged tanks were available from depots, including 26 "Turm 38(t) (W)" from Heereszeugamt Wien (Vienna) and 100 "Turm 38(t) (P)" from Heereskraftfahrzeug Werkstatt Pschelautsch (Prelouc). Due to the availability of some turrets without their guns, another version called the PzKpfw-Turm 38(t) Behelfsmäßig f.2 MG.37 (t) was developed, which had a second 7.92mm MG.37 in place of the main gun. Although there were plans to complete 84 of these in 1944, only four are known to have been deployed in Festung Bruenn (Brno) in April 1945.

About 30 of the *Drehtürm* 38(t) fortifications were deployed along the *Südwall* on the French Mediterranean coast, including this one on the Promenade des Anglais in Nice.

The table below indicates the disposition of the turrets based on a March 1945 report. The turrets listed for the *Atlantikwall* in fact went to the *Südwall* on the French Mediterranean coast, mainly to Marseilles and Toulon. It seems likely that some of the turrets allotted elsewhere on the Mediterranean coast in fact ended up in France, since tallies of the fortifications on the *Südwall* show that there were at least 30 assigned to the French Mediterranean coast and eight more to the Pyrenees. Many of the turrets emplaced on the Greek islands remained in Greek service through much of the Cold War.

The prototype of the PzKpfw-Turm 38(t) Behelfsmäßig f.2 MG.37 (t) *Drehtürm* during trials at the Hillersleben artillery proving ground. This version lacked the usual 37mm gun, substituting a second machine gun, which is not fitted in this view. Only four of these were deployed in the fortifications around Brno in the final weeks of World War II.

Panzer 38 (t) Drehtürm deployment

Norway	75
Denmark	20
Atlantikwall/France	9
Italy	25
Yugoslavia/Greece	150
Eastern Front	78

When the Bulgarian People's Army retired its handful of PzKpfw 38(t) in the 1950s, they were converted into bunkers on the southern border with Greece. In the early 1960s when Sweden's obsolete Stridsvagen m/41 were converted into turretless armored personnel carriers, the spare turrets were used to create defensive positions around important military facilities such as airbases. These emplaced turret bunkers remained in service well into the 1980s.

The PzKpfw 38(t) neue Ausführung was a complete redesign of the PzKpfw 38(t), intended to satisfy a German reconnaissance-tank requirement. Although rejected in favor of the Luchs, the chassis served as the basis for the later Jagdpanzer 38 Hetzer.

Next Generation: PzKfw 38(t) n.A.

The Surin design team at BMM had been working on a next-generation version of the PzKpfw 38(t) since 1939. This was originally intended to replace the PzKpfw 38(t) on the production lines in the autumn of 1942. The prospects for continued production of the PzKpfw 38(t) as a battle tank came into increasing doubt by early 1942 due to the inadequate performance of the 37mm gun against the new Soviet tanks. In the meantime, another application for the tank had emerged.

In July 1940, the Waffenamt circulated a requirement for a light reconnaissance tank to three tank plants: BMM, Škoda, and MAN.

BMM offered its new-generation PzKpfw 38(t), called variously the Praga TNH n.A., PzKpfw 38(t) n.A. (neue Ausführung: new version), or PzSpWg II Ausf. BMM. It was armed with the improved 37mm Škoda A19 gun, and was powered by a 220hp Praga NR gasoline engine. Armor was 50mm on the gun mantlet, 30mm on other front panels, and 25mm on the sides. The first of five prototypes was completed in April 1942 and sent to the Kummersdorf proving ground for trials against the Škoda T-15 and the MAN VK 1303. The Czech designs were faulted for having a shorter range than their German rival, and the 37mm gun meant a very crowded turret interior compared with the smaller 20mm gun in the VK 1303. Curiously enough, there were plans to re-equip all three designs with a 50mm gun in spite of the complaints about the limited space with the smaller 37mm gun. Czech accounts indicate that the test board favored the BMM tank, in no small measure due to its robust power train. This vehicle later served as the automotive basis for the Jagdpanzer 38(t) Hetzer.

The failure of the rival Luchs reconnaissance-tank program led to the production of 70 Aufklärungspanzer 38 (2cm) based on the PzKpfw 38(t) Ausf. M (10.Serie) chassis.

F

TANKS OF THE NEUTRAL POWERS

1: PZW 39, ZUG.7, 7.DIVISION, SWISS ARMY, TOGGENBURG, 1941

The LTL-H (Pzw 39) initially were deployed in platoon strength with six of the Swiss infantry divisions (1, 2, 4, 5, 6, 7). The initial camouflage scheme was a two-color camouflage of *Feldgrau* (field gray) and *Gelbolive* (olive green), although in later years, a three-color scheme sometimes was used.

The Swiss tank platoons were assigned various platoon insignia: playing cards, rhinoceros, snake, crayfish, turtle, and crocodile. In this case, it is the crocodile insignia of Zug.7. To avoid confusion near the borders, in October 1940 orders were formulated for applying neutrality identity markings (*Zeigen für die Kenntlichmachung*). On tanks, this consisted of the national code "CH" (Confoederatio Helvetica) painted in large yellow letters on the front, side, and top of the tank. Registration plates were fitted on the front and rear, consisting of overall black lacquer plate with white serial numbers, and the national crest in red with a white cross and the letter "M" (*militar*) in red. The tanks of Zug.7 were numbered 7571 to 7574. Later, Zug.7 was amalgamated with Zug.6 to form the new Pzw.Kp. I, attached to the 1.Leichte Brigade headquartered in Morges Jura.

2: STRIDSVAGEN STRV M/41 SI, PANSARREGEMENTE P3, 10 SÖDERMANLANDS PANSERBRIGAD, STRÄGNARÄ, SWEDEN, 1943

Prior to World War II, Swedish tanks were generally finished in field gray (*Fältgrå*), which was a true gray and not the usual gray-green. In 1941, the army issued "Arméorder nr 155," which established a new multi-color camouflage system. The usual pattern for tanks consisted of a base color of *Olivgrön* (olive green) with patches of *Gulbrun* (yellow brown), *Grå* (gray), and *Svart* (black). These were usually spray-painted and did not follow a fixed pattern.

Tactical markings usually consisted of a three-digit number on the rear turret side in white outline. This was the last three digits of the army registration number (*Militärnummer*) rather than the usual company/platoon/tank system. In the case of the original SI series of tanks, the registration numbers were 199 to 314; this example shows tank number 268. In the case of the second batch of SII tanks, the numbers were 80001 to 80104, simplified by dropping the "80" prefix. So typical numbers were in the pattern of "068" or "102." National markings were carried in the form of a Swedish flag painted on the hull's side.

1

7571

2

269

An Aufklärüngspanzer 38 (2cm) in a tank graveyard at the Bory airfield outside Plzen (Pilsen) shortly after the conclusion of the war in May 1945. As can be seen, the forward superstructure hull was more elevated than on the normal gun tanks, in order to accommodate the *Hängelafette* turret.

In the event, the MAN VK 1303 was selected for production. The plans originally called for the production of 800 PzSpWg II Luchs (Lynx) but this was later trimmed back to only 100 tanks due to fundamental design flaws. The Luchs suffered from a delicate steering system, which left most of the inventory inoperative through 1943 and only marginally serviceable in 1944–45. There were seldom more than two dozen of the type in service at any given time.

The failure of the Luchs program left the Wehrmacht without its intended scout tank, so in the summer of 1943, the Waffenamt approached BMM about adapting the PzKpfw 38(t) chassis to this role. At the time, BMM production was focused on the Ausf. M (10.Serie), which had a center-mounted engine for the various self-propelled-gun versions. This required a reconfiguration back to the tank layout with the engine in the rear. Since the Aufklärüngspanzer was intended to perform the same role as existing wheeled (SdKfz. 234/1) and half-track (Sd.Kfz.250/9) scout vehicles, it was configured around the standard 20mm *Hängelafette* turret. A total of 70 Aufklärüngspanzer 38 (2cm) were manufactured in February and March 1944. They were deployed in early 1944 with Panzergrenadier Division Grossdeutschland and 3.Panzer-Division. There was a scheme to develop a scout version with the short 75mm gun as a parallel to half-tracked vehicles such as the SdKfz 250/8 and SdKfz 251/9 and wheeled scout vehicles such as the SdKfz 234/3. Although two prototypes were built in 1944, it was not accepted for production, presumably due to the higher priority afforded to the new Jagdpanzer 38 (Hetzer) assault gun.

EXPORT PzKpfw 38(t)

Sweden

After the Wehrmacht took over the Swedish tank order at the BMM plant, the Swedish Army continued in its quest to obtain the TNH-Sv (Sv = Svensk). The German government refused to divert BMM production capacity for such exports, so license production was offered as an alternative. Scania-Vabis was assigned as the Swedish manufacturer, and various components such as a Scania-Vabis engine were provided to BMM for incorporation into a modified prototype. In early 1941, BMM transferred manufacturing plans and assembly jigs to Sweden and the TNH-Sv prototype was shipped from BMM in late May 1941. The Swedish version was designated as Strv m/41 (*Stridsvagen*: combat vehicle) and a total of 116 tanks were built. These were deployed with the Södermanlands Pansarregemente P3 in Strägnarä, later incorporated into the 10 Södermanlands Panserbrigad in early 1943. The Swedish tanks were powered by a Scania-Vabis L1664/13, offering 140hp. In comparison to the Czech-manufactured tanks, the Swedish turret had a flat roof over the rear bustle. The armament was a 37mm Bofors m/38 gun.

This program was successful enough that the Swedish Army decided to acquire a second series of 122 tanks in the improved Strv m/41 SII configuration as part of the effort to equip all three army corps with a tank brigade. The initial version was retroactively designated as the Strv m/41 SI. The SII version introduced thicker frontal armor, increasing from 25mm to 50mm, and so necessitating a more powerful L-603 160hp engine. The chassis was lengthened to accommodate the new engine and improvements were made to the turret. The second batch was delivered from October 1943 to March 1944, principally to Skaraborgs Pansarregemente P4 in Skövde. In the event, only 104 tanks were delivered of the 122 ordered. The remaining chassis were used as the basis for the Sav m/43 10.5cm assault gun. The Strv m/41 SI and SII tanks remained in Swedish Army service in dwindling numbers until 1957. Some were used as the basis for other self-propelled guns, but 220 were rebuilt into the Pvb 301 armored personnel carrier in 1960–63, which kept the chassis in service into the early 1970s. As mentioned above, the turrets were recycled as static-defense pillboxes.

The Saab-Scania Stridsvagen m/41 S-I had many small detail differences to the PzKpfw 38(t), including a second periscopic sight on the roof for the loader, and an extended turret bustle with flat turret roof.

Slovakia

While Berlin refused to export new tanks to neutrals such as Sweden, it made some modest exceptions for allied armies such as Slovakia. After the Slovak participation in the 1939 invasion of Poland alongside the Wehrmacht, the Slovak Army hoped to build up its armored force along the lines of the original Czechoslovak Fast Divisions. Berlin was reluctant to supply so many tanks while still creating its own new panzer divisions, but allowed a contract to be signed in April 1940. The delivery of these ten LT-38 tanks to the armored regiment in Martin was completed on February 10, 1941; a second contract for a further 20 LT-38 tanks was signed in September 1940 and delivered in June 1942. The BMM plant still had a batch of 21 unarmed LTL light tanks on the factory grounds that had been built for Latvia but never delivered. BMM proposed to arm these with the usual Škoda A7 37mm gun instead of the intended 20mm Oerlikon with the designation changed to LTS. Slovakia purchased these and they were delivered in November 1940 ahead of the LT-38; they were designated as LT-40 in Slovak service. In the event, these tanks were not yet armed, so seven of these had their gun apertures plated over and used as command tanks for Operation *Barbarossa* in June 1941. The remainder were armed in December 1941 and gradually sent to the Russian front.

The ten LT-38 and seven LT-40 command tanks were used alongside 30 older LT-35 tanks to form a tank battalion (Kobornia) under the Slovak Mobile Group organized for participation in the Russian campaign. The Mobile Group took part in the 1941 invasion of the Soviet Union, fighting along the southern route from Lvov to Kiev. In July, it was expanded into a Mobile Brigade, and the tank element expanded into a tank regiment as additional tanks became available. In late August, it was elevated to a Mobile Division, but by this time most of its tanks were worn out and had been returned to Slovakia for repairs. Two platoons of tanks returned to the Russian front in late October, serving in the campaign in southern Russia and the Crimea, but losing most of their tanks in the January–February 1942 fighting. The Mobile Division was formally redesignated as an infantry division in August 1943 after its heavy losses in the Crimea. Slovakia attempted to purchase additional LT-38 tanks to make up for combat losses, but was rebuffed several times by Berlin. In June 1943, Berlin finally

G

1: LT-38, SLOVAK FAST BRIGADE, UKRAINE, JULY 1941

The first five LT-38 were delivered to the Slovak Army in their original three-color Czechoslovak scheme of *tmave zelene* (dark green), *okrove zlute* (ochre yellow), and *zemite hnede* (earth brown), such as here (V-3003). In subsequent years, they were repainted in the standard Czechoslovak Army olive drab (khaki). The two companies of LT-38 that took part in the 1941 invasion of the Soviet Union had the tactical numbers 211–215 and 311–315. Some tanks had the double-arm Slovak cross in white, as seen here. Later batches of PzKpfw 38(t) were delivered in standard German colors, either dark gray or, later, dark yellow.

2: LT-40, SLOVAK MOBILE DIVISION, CAUCASUS CAMPAIGN, NOVEMBER 1942

The delay in arming the Latvian LTL tanks meant that most were not deployed with the Slovak forces on the Russian Front until 1942. This is one of the tanks deployed with a reinforcing tank company that arrived in November 1942. The actual finish of these tanks is not clear due to a lack of records. In some cases they are depicted in overall Czech olive drab (khaki), but more recent depictions lean towards the use of standard German dark gray, as shown here. In May 1942, the Slovak Army shifted its national insignia to a tri-color shield as seen here instead of the Slovak cross used earlier.

1

2

The Slovak Army purchased ten LT-38 light tanks from BMM from the early production batches.

consented to an order for 57 tanks, but since the PzKpfw 38(t) was no longer in production, these came from German stockpiles at the Vienna depot. The first were delivered in August 1943 and a total of 37 were received at the time of the last delivery in July 1944. These were an extremely mixed bag of types, including all variants from Ausf. A to Ausf. G. Some of these tanks took part in the Slovak Uprising against the Germans in August 1944.

Hungary

The Hungarian Honvéd (army) took part in the invasion of the Soviet Union in 1941, and deployed its Fast Corps, which included 60 Ansaldo L3 tankettes and 81 Toldi light tanks. These tanks were obsolete in modern battlefield conditions, but Germany proved very reluctant to sell any modern tanks such as the PzKpfw III or PzKpfw IV. The Honvéd settled on buying 102 PzKpfw 38(t) Ausf. F and Ausf. G from German stocks. The PzKpfw 38(t) was known as the Škoda T-38 in Hungarian service, and these were delivered from November 1941 to March 1942 to create the new 1.páncélos hadosztály (1st Armored Division). Three more PzKpfw 38(t) Ausf. C were also transferred from German stocks later in the year. The 1st Armored Division began to encounter the Red Army in a series of battles along the Don River beginning on July 18, 1942. Contact with Soviet T-34 and KV tank units made it abundantly clear that the 37mm gun on the PzKpfw 38(t) was completely inadequate, and nearly half the T-38 tanks were lost in combat in the 1942 fighting. The 1st Armored Division was holding a sector of the Don front north of Stalingrad at the time of the Soviet offensive on January 12, 1943. It fought as part of the German Korps Cramer alongside two German infantry divisions. The division retreated from the Uryv bridgehead about 70km back from its initial positions towards Noviy Oskol and Korotscha. Its attempt to create a defensive line failed and the division was forced into another fighting withdrawal back to the Donets River near Belgorod on February 8, 1943. The Don battles destroyed the Hungarian 2nd Army but the 1st Armored Division was the only division to emerge partially intact. It lost its entire inventory of T-38 tanks except for a few that had remained behind in Hungary for training.

Romania

Romania license-produced the Škoda LT-35 as the R-2, and this was one of its principal tanks at the time of the invasion of the Soviet Union in June 1941. The Romanian armored force was largely destroyed in the 1942 fighting that culminated in the disastrous Stalingrad campaign. The collapse of the ill-equipped Romanian Army formations was a central cause in the collapse of the Stalingrad front, and forced the Germans to reconsider their miserly arms policy. As the first stage in rebuilding the Romanian Army, the Germans began the Birnbaum Program, under which 50 worn-out PzKpfw 38(t) light tanks were shipped directly to Romanian units in the Kuban bridgehead in March 1943. These were mostly old tanks from the 22.Panzer-Division and its successor units. They formed an independent tank battalion (Batalionul carelor de lupta T-38) but less than half the tanks were functional and it took time to repair the remainder. This unit saw extensive fighting in the Kuban region, on the Azov Sea near Kerch, and on the Perekop peninsula leading into Crimea. It was withdrawn to Sevastopol in April 1944 and sent back to Romania with only a handful of its original tanks.

Following the decimation of Romanian tank units near Stalingrad in January 1943, Berlin delivered 50 obsolete PzKpfw 38(t) light tanks to an independent Romanian tank battalion, which used them in the fighting in the Kuban region in 1943.

The 9th Company of the Bulgarian Tank Brigade operating ten "Lek Tank Praga," which were obtained from Germany in 1943. One is seen here on parade in Sofia after participating in the campaign in Yugoslavia with the allied Red Army. Seven of these remained in service into the 1950s.

Bulgaria

Unlike most of Germany's eastern allies, Bulgaria refused to take part in the invasion of Russia in 1941. As a result, Germany refused to provide anything more than token equipment upgrades in 1941–43. In May 1943, Germany provided ten PzKpfw 38(t) from its own stocks, which included a mish-mash of types including some old Ausf. A, B, C, E, F, and G. These served in the 9.Rota (9th Company) of the Tankova Brigada (Tank Brigade). When Bulgaria switched sides in September 1944, this unit took part in combat against the Wehrmacht alongside the Red Army.

POSTWAR CZECHOSLOVAK SERVICE

After World War II, the new Czechoslovak Army collected a large number of abandoned German armored vehicles with plans to rehabilitate some of them for domestic use or for export. A total of about 50 PzKpfw 38(t) tanks were located, some of them ex-Slovak tanks and some in workshops. Of these, 31 were put back in running order and designated as LT-38/37, the "/37" indicating the 37mm gun. They were deployed with the 21. and 22. tankové brigády with the 1.motorizované divize in Prague and the 3. motorizované divize in Hodonín. They remained in service into the 1950s, when they were replaced by Soviet equipment. At least two were still in service as training tanks with the Jan Žižka military school in Trocnov as late as 1959.

The Czechoslovak armaments industry hoped to re-establish itself in the world export market after World War II, and the ČKD company began offering armored vehicles for international sale. The first success came in 1946 when a deal was signed with Switzerland for the production of 100 Jagdpanzer 38 Hetzer assault guns as the Panzerjäger G 13. A deal to sell 20 new AH-IVb tankettes and 20 LTP light tanks to Bolivia fell through for political reasons, but 20 new Praga AH-IV Hb tankettes were sold to Ethiopia in 1950. There was some hope to sell a light reconnaissance tank based on the Jagdpanzer 38 chassis to Switzerland and other export clients, armed with a new Škoda 57mm gun. A mock-up of this tank, known as the TNH-57, was built in 1949 on the fifth prototype of the surviving PzKpfw 38(t) n.A prototype. The front hull superstructure was widened to permit an enlarged turret race, and a new and larger turret was developed. This project eventually fell into limbo after the Communist takeover of the Czechoslovak government, and the Soviet insistence that the Czechoslovak defense industry manufacture Soviet weapons under license. Andrej Surin, who had designed the PzKpfw 38(t), led the program to adapt the Soviet T-34-85 tank to Czechoslovak manufacture at ČKD and the new ZVJS plant in Martin starting in 1953. So ended independent Czechoslovak tank design.

The fifth PzKpfw 38(t) neue Ausführung prototype was rebuilt as the TNH-57 light tank in 1949 in hopes of soliciting export interest. In the event, the rise of the Communist government put an end to independent Czechoslovak tank development before production could start. This illustration shows the intended configuration of the tank.

FURTHER READING

The PzKpfw 38(t) has been well covered in existing literature, with the various Francev books providing comprehensive coverage from multiple aspects of its development and use. The Jentz/Doyle monograph provides a more detailed technical account strictly from the German perspective.

Panzerkampfwagen 38 (t): Gerätebeschreibung und Bedienungsanweisung zum Fahrgestell (Waffenamt: 1942)

Baadstöe, Christer (ed.), *Svenskt pansar under beredskapstiden 1939–1945* (SPFH: 1992)

Baryatinskiy, Mikhail, *Legkiy tank Pz.38(t)* (Bronekollektsiya #4: 2004)

Francev, Vladimir, *Československé Tankové Síly 1945–1992* (Grada: 2012)

Francev, Vladimir, *Exportní Lehké Tanky Praga* (MBI: 2007)

Francev, Vladimir, *Exportní Tančíky Praga* (MBI: 2004)

Francev, Vladimir, *PzKpfw 38(t) Ausf. A–D in Detail* (Wings and Wheels: 2006)

Francev, Vladimir and Charles Kliment, *Praga LT vz. 38* (MBI: 1997)

Jentz, Thomas and Hilary Doyle, *Panzerkampfwagen 38(t)* (Panzertracts: 2007)

Kalinin, Aleksey, *Panzerkampfwagen 38 (t): Konstruirovanie i proizvodstvo* (World of Tanks: 2013)

Kliment, Charles, *PzKpfw 38(t) Variations* (Squadron-Signal: 2013)

Kliment, Charles and Hilary Doyle, *PzKpfw 38(t) in Action* (Squadron-Signal: 1979)

Kliment, Charles and Vladimir Francev, *Czechoslovak Armored Fighting Vehicles 1918–1948* (Schiffer: 1997)

Ledwoch, Janusz, *LT vz. 34/40 TNH* (Wyd. Militaria: 2000)

Ledwoch, Janusz, *PzKfw 38(t): Tank Power Vol. 21* (Wyd. Militaria: 2006)

Sallaz, Kurt and Peter Riklin, *Bewaffnung und Ausrüstung der Schweizer Armee seit 1817: panzer und Panzerabwehr* (Stocker-Schmid: 1982)

Speilberger, Walter, *Panzers 35(t) and 38(t) and their Variants 1920–1945* (Schiffer: 2008)

Stapfer, Hans-Heiri, Panzer *38(t)/Swiss LTL-H Walk-Around* (Squadron Signal: 2009)

Zöllner, Markus, Panzer *38(t): Wehrmacht Special No 4012* (Tankograd: 2008)

INDEX

References in **bold** refer to figures and illustrations

ammunition 14, **15**
antitank guns 12, 14, **14**, 25
antitank rifles 12, 25
armored trains **33**, **34**, **35** (34)

BMM 11, 21, 24, 28, 37–38, 40, 41
Bulgaria 46, **46**

camouflage *see* markings and insignia
casualties 20
ČKD 5, 6, 10, 11, 24, 46–47
Czechoslovak Army, tank
   requirements 10
Czechoslovakia 4
   arms industry 5, 10, 46–47
   German occupation 10
   tank exports 5–9

Drehtürm 36–37, **36**, **37**

Fall Blau 30, 31–34
flotation systems **21**
France 16–20
French Army
   1e DCR 18
   25e BCC 17–18
   28e BCC 17–18

German Army
   2.leichte-Division 16
   3.leichte-Division 12, 16
   Gruppe Michalik 32
   Kampfgruppe Koll 30
   Kampfgruppe Rodt 31
   panzer units
      1.Panzer-Division 30
      2.Panzer-Division 30
      5.Panzer-Division 18
      7.Panzer-Division 16, 17, **17**, **19** (18), 20, 26, 30
      8.Panzer-Division 16, 17, 20, 24
      12.Panzer-Division 30
      20.Panzer-Division 26
      22.Panzer-Division 30, 31, **31**, 32–33
   Panzer-Abteilung.67 11–12, **13**, **19** (18)
   Panzer-Regiment.10 17
   Panzer-Regiment.25 17, **17**, 20, **24**
   Panzer-Regiment.204 31, **31**, 32

half-tracks 40
Heeres Waffenamt 10, 13, 28–29, 37, 40
Hungary 44, **45**

Imperial Mechanized Brigade (Iran)
   regiments
      1st Antiaircraft Regiment 6
      2nd AFV Regiment 6, 8
      3rd Mechanized Infantry Regiment 6
insignia *see* markings and insignia
Iran 5–6

Latvia 6

machine guns 14, 28
markings and insignia 9 (8), **19** (18), **27** (26), **33**, **35** (34), **39** (38), **43** (42)
mines 25

Operation *Barbarossa* 24–25
Operation *Braunschweig* 32
Operation *Bustard Hunt* 31
Operation *Fredidericus II* 32
Operation *Marita* 24
Operation *Uranus* 32
Operation *Wilhelm* 32

Panzerträgerwagen **33**, 34
Peru 7–8
Polish campaign 12, **19** (18)
PzKpfw 38(t) 4–5, **11**
   ammunition 14, **15**
   as anti-partisan tanks 34, **35** (34)
   AP-1 flotation system **21**
   armor 13, 20, 21, 25, 28, 38
   Aufklärungspanzer 38 (2cm) version 38, 40, **40**
   Ausf. A 11, **11**, 13, **19** (18), **36**
   Ausf. B 13, **16**, **17**
   Ausf. C 13, **13**, **24**, 33
   Ausf. D 13, 20
   Ausf. E **4**, **20**, 21, 33
   Ausf. F 21, **21**, **22–23** (22), **27** (26), **32**, 44, **45**
   Ausf. G 28–29, **29**, **35** (34), 44, 45
   Ausf. M (10. Serie) 40
   Ausf. S 24, **25**
   in Bulgaria 46, **46**
   combat debut 11–12
   compared with Soviet tanks 25
   crew layout 13–14, **13**
   decline of 30, 33–34
   deployment and losses **29**
   durability 25–26, **26**, 33
   early revisions 13
   engine 16
   exhaust muffler 11, **11**, 21
   exports 41–46
   Fall Blau 31–34
   final production types 28–29, **29**, **30**
   in France 16–20
   guns 14, **14**, 28, 37, 38, 44
   hull construction 21, **21**, 24
   in Hungary 44, **45**
   late production versions 20–23
   LT 38/37 version 46
   LT 38 version (Slovakia) 4, 10–11, 42, **43** (42), **44**
   LT 40 version (Slovakia) 42, **43** (42)
   markings and insignia **19** (18), **27** (26), **33**, **35** (34)
   postwar Czechoslovak service 46–47
   PzKpfw 38(t) n.A. 37–38, **37**, **47**
   radios and antenna 11, 12, 15, **15**
   in Romania 45, **45**
   Russian Front 24–28, 30
   in Slovakia 42–44, **43** (42), **44**
   stowage bins 14
   Stridsvagen Strv m/41 version (Sweden) **39** (38), 41, **41**
   suspension 21
   in Sweden **39** (38), 41, **41**

technical description 13–16
TNH-57 light tank 47, **47**
turrets **14**, 21, 24, 28, 36–37, **36**, **37**
variants **16**
winter performance 26, 28
see also tanks

radios and antenna **11**, **12**, 13, 15, **15**, **19** (18)
road wheels 5, 6
Romania 45, **45**
Rommel, Erwin 17
Russian Front 24–28, 30

Scania-Vabis 41
Škoda 5, 10, 37, 38, 44, 45, 47
Slovakia 42–44, **43** (42), **44**
Soviet Army
   47th Army 32
   55th Tank Brigade 32
   229th Separate Tank Battalion 32
Surin, Alexej 5
suspension 5, **6**, 21
Sweden 24, **41**, **39** (38), 41
Switzerland **39** (38)

tanks
   AH-IV tankette 5, 6, 46–47
   BT-7 25
   Char B1 bis 17
   durability **26**
   exports 5–9
   Hotchkiss H39 16, 17, 34
   Jagdpanzer 38 46, 47
   KV 4, 25, 32
   losses 20, 25, 26, **26**, **29**
   LT 34 5, **6**
   LT 35 10
   LTH 6
   LTL **6**, 42
   LTL-H (PZW 39) 7, 8, **39** (38)
   LTM 38 11
   LTP 7–8, **7**, **9** (8)
   MAN VK 1303 38, 40
   Panzerbefelswagen 38(t) **12**
   Panzerwagen 39 8, **8**
   PzBef.38(t) 17
   PzKpfw 35(t) 10
   PzKpfw I 10, 16, 25, 28
   PzKpfw II 10, 11, 12, 16
   PzKpfw III 10, 25, 26
   PzKpfw III(t) 11, 12
   PzKpfw IV 16, 25, 26
   PzSpWg II Luchs 40
   Renault FT 34
   Renault R35 16
   Somua S35 34
   Soviet capture of 28
   T-26 25, 31
   T-34 4, 25, 30
   T-60 31
   Tančik vz. 30 5
   TNH light tank 5, **5**, **9** (8)
   TNH-S 10
   TNH-Sv 24, 41
   see also PzKpfw 38(t)

Unternehmen Trappenjagd 31

AGAINST FREUD